Reading Essentials®
in Social Studies

U.S. GOVERNMENT

D1604801

The Executive Branch

Carol Parenzan Smalley

PERFECTION LEARNING®

EDITORIAL DIRECTOR	Susan C. Thies
EDITORS	Lucy Miller, Judith A. Bates
DESIGN DIRECTOR	Randy Messer
BOOK DESIGN	Emily J. Greazel
COVER DESIGN	Michael Aspengren

IMAGE CREDITS

Associated Press: pp. 19, 25, 42; © Greg Smith/CORBIS SABA: pp. 4–5; © Wally McNamee/CORBIS: p. 12; © James L. Amos/CORBIS: p. 30; © Chase Swift/CORBIS: p. 35; © Bettmann/CORBIS: p. 37; © Christopher J. Morris/CORBIS: p. 40

Corel Professional Photos: back cover, front cover (bottom left), pp. 42–43; Electronic Clipper/Liquid Library: p. 28; John F. Kennedy Library: p. 21; Library of Congress: pp. 7, 14, 15, 16, 17, 23, 24, 33, 47; Map Resources: p. 9; NARA: front cover (bottom center), pp. 10, 11 (top), 27; Perfection Learning: pp. 29, 43; Photos.com: front cover (main, bottom left), pp. 1, 11 (bottom), 22, 26, 31, 32, 34, 41

Some images ClipArt.com, Photos.com, NARA, Library of Congress: (Chapter heading bar) pp. 3, 4, 9, 12, 25, 36, 41, 44–45

A special thanks to William J. Miller, attorney, for reviewing this book

Perfection Learning® Corporation
1000 North Second Avenue, P.O. Box 500
Logan, Iowa 51546-0500.
Tel: 1-800-831-4190 • Fax: 1-800-543-2745
perfectionlearning.com

1 2 3 4 5 6 PP 09 08 07 06 05 04

ISBN 0-7891-6242-3

Contents

The Executive Branch at a Glance

General Facts

Head of the Executive Branch president

Salary of the President (2003) $400,000

First President George Washington

Official Presidential Residence/Office
The White House in Washington, D.C.

Minimum Age of the President 35

Sets of Related Presidents 4
Franklin Delano Roosevelt and Theodore Roosevelt (cousins), John Adams and John Quincy Adams (father and son), William Henry Harrison and Benjamin Harrison (grandfather and grandson), and George Bush and George W. Bush (father and son)

Salary of the Vice President (2003)
$198,600

Number of Permanent Cabinet Members (2003)
16—vice president, attorney general, and 14 secretaries

Additions to the Cabinet

Under President George W. Bush, cabinet-level rank was given to the chief of staff, the administrator of the Environmental Protection Agency (EPA), the director of the Office of Management and Budget, the director of the National Drug Control **Policy**, and the U.S. Trade representative. President Bush also created the Department of Homeland Security, whose director joined the cabinet as well.

Timeline of Important Events

1789   Congress changes the name of the Department of Foreign Affairs to the Department of State, making it the first cabinet-level department.

The Department of the Treasury is the second executive department created by the first Congress.

Congress sets up the third executive department, the Department of War, to handle military affairs.

Congress creates the Office of the Attorney General. The attorney general serves on the cabinet but does not head a department.

1798   Congress separates the naval forces from the Department of War and forms the Department of the Navy and makes it part of the cabinet.

1849   The Department of the Interior is established by Congress and becomes part of the cabinet.

George W. Bush (left), forty-third president of the United States and George Bush (right), forty-first president of the United States

5

1862	The United States Department of Agriculture (USDA) is created by Congress. The head of the department is not a member of the cabinet.
1867	Congress sets up a non-cabinet agency called the Department of Education, which later becomes part of the Department of the Interior.
1870	Because of the many legal problems that arose from the Civil War, the Department of Justice is established by Congress as part of the cabinet, headed by the attorney general.
1884	Congress establishes the Bureau of Labor as part of the Department of the Interior.
1888	The Department of Labor becomes independent from the Department of the Interior, but the department head is not a cabinet member.
1889	The USDA becomes a member of the cabinet as the Department of Agriculture.
1903	Congress sets up the Department of Commerce and Labor as a member of the cabinet.
1913	The Department of Labor and the Department of Commerce become separate executive departments serving on the cabinet.
1920	Congress creates the Veterans Bureau to serve the needs of **veterans**. This is not a cabinet post.
1930	Congress combines the Veterans Bureau with several other agencies to form the Veterans Administration (VA), which is not part of the cabinet.
1934	Congress establishes the Federal Housing Administration (FHA) to provide mortgage insurance programs.

1939	The Federal Security Agency is established as an independent agency to handle welfare services formerly provided by state and local governments. The Department of Education is moved here and renamed the Office of Education.
1947	All branches of the armed forces unite to become the National Military Establishment (NME).
	The Presidential Succession Act becomes law.
1949	The NME becomes part of the cabinet as the Department of Defense.
1951	The 22nd Amendment to the Constitution states that no person shall be elected president more than twice.
1953	The Federal Security Agency becomes the Department of Health, Education, and Welfare (HEW) and a cabinet member.
1965	Congress combines the FHA and other like agencies into the Department of Housing and Urban Development (HUD) to solve housing and community problems created by fast-growing cities.

FHA low Income housing project,
Holyoke, Massachusetts, 1940s

1965	The 25th Amendment to the Constitution states that if there is a vacancy in the vice presidency, the president shall nominate a vice president. To be **confirmed**, there must be a majority vote of both houses of Congress. If the president is unable to perform his duties, his powers are transferred to the vice president until the president is able to resume the duties of his office.
1966	The Department of **Transportation** is established, combining transportation agencies from other departments.
1977	The Department of Energy is established, pulling together energy-related agencies scattered throughout the government.
1979	The Department of Education is established as a separate cabinet position. HEW is renamed the Department of Health and Human Services.
1988	The Department of Veterans Affairs is established, taking over responsibilities of the VA. The secretary of the department becomes a member of the cabinet.
2001	The Office of Homeland Security is created in response to the terrorist attacks on September 11.
2002	The Office of Homeland Security becomes the Department of Homeland Security and a cabinet member.

Chapter 1

Discontent Brings Change

The history of United States government began in the early 1600s, when citizens of Great Britain sailed across the Atlantic Ocean and established colonies along the eastern coast of the North American continent. These colonists were still considered citizens of Great Britain and were ruled by the British monarchy.

By the mid-1700s, 13 colonies were in place. The colonists, however, were **discontent**. They were living under the king's rule while forging a new life in a new land. So the colonists opted to fight for their freedom. This march for independence led to the founding of the United States of America.

New Hampshire

Massachusetts

New York

Rhode Island

Connecticut

Pennsylvania

New Jersey

Delaware

Virginia

Maryland

North Carolina

South Carolina

Georgia

The 13 colonies

American Revolutionary War

The colonists declared war against Great Britain. In 1775, fighting began with battles in Lexington and Concord, Massachusetts. Today we refer to this war as the American Revolutionary War. After eight years of intense battle, the colonists emerged victorious. The king no longer controlled the colonies, and the United States was born. The country's statement of independence, drafted in 1776, was now in effect.

Declaration of Independence

To formally declare their intent for freedom and their discontent with British rule, representatives of the colonies penned the Declaration of Independence in 1776. Thomas Jefferson, who wrote the first draft of the document in three parts, spearheaded this effort.

The Declaration centered on the concept of democracy, a form of government in which the people rule. Using phrases such as "all men are created equal," the **preamble**, or first part, laid the foundation for the rest of the document.

Because the colonists were dissatisfied with King George III, the second section of the Declaration formally listed the colonists' complaints against the ruler.

The third and final part of this history-changing document declared that the 13 colonies were free of Britain's rule. Fifty-six representatives from the 13 colonies signed the final draft of the document.

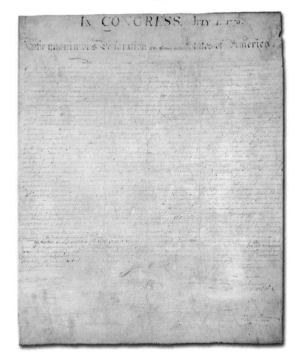

The original Declaration of Independence, now exhibited in the rotunda of the National Archives Building in Washington, D.C.

Constitution

By 1783, the colonists had freed themselves from a ruler who held all the power. They wanted a new government that had a system of **checks and balances**—one in which power could not be held by a single person or single area of government. The colonies needed a government to aid them, not rule them.

In 1787, after many years of ongoing debate, the new country crafted a document that set down the principles for the government. That document, the Constitution of the United States, still guides the nation today.

The framers of the Constitution provided for three coequal branches of government—the **executive branch**, the **legislative branch**, and the **judicial branch**. All three branches form a system of checks and balances. The branches work together in order for the government to be effective.

Constructing a Three-Legged Stool

Have you ever sat on a three-legged stool? What happens if one leg of the stool is longer than the other two by just an inch or so? People or objects perched on the seat find it hard not to tip. Why? The stool is out of balance.

The three branches of the U.S. government are very similar to this three-legged stool. When one branch has more power than the other two, the item at the top—in this case the citizens of the United States—feels out of balance and a correction must be made. That's the purpose of checks and balances—to keep the power of government level.

Chapter 2

One of Three Government Legs

The executive branch ensures that the laws of the United States are obeyed. This branch is composed of the president, vice president, the cabinet, the Executive Office, and independent agencies. Each plays an important role in this branch of government. Most executive offices are in the White House and in the Eisenhower Executive Office Building on the White House grounds in Washington, D.C. The president's office is called the Oval Office and is the center of executive-branch activity.

The Oval Office in Washington, D.C.

The President

Hail to the Chief

The president of the United States heads the executive branch of government and is sometimes called the *chief executive*. In many ways, the president acts like the chief executive officer (CEO) of a large corporation. He surrounds himself with experts and consults his "board of directors"—the cabinet. His actions are checked by the two other branches of government—the legislative branch and the judicial branch.

U.S. Census Bureau POPClock

So how many people do the president's actions and decisions affect? According to the U.S. Bureau of the Census, more than 292 million people resided in the United States in 2003. The number of United States residents changes every few seconds. Want to know what the estimated number is right now? Visit the Bureau's POPClock at **www.census.gov/cgi-bin/popclock**.

Being president of the United States is a tough job. Compared to the large salaries paid to most CEOs, the president's salary of $400,000 a year is meager for what is expected of him. The president's actions and decisions affect each and every person in the country.

Who Can Be President?

Perhaps one day you can be president of the United States. The Constitution states that in order to be president, a person must be at least 35 years old and a natural-born citizen of the United States.

In 2001, George W. Bush, the forty-third president, was sworn into office for a four-year term. He is the son of George Bush, the country's forty-first president. Nicknamed "W" to distinguish him from his father, George W. Bush was born in 1946, making him 54 years old the day he became president.

Presidents

	President	Term	Party	Vice President(s)
1	George Washington	1789–1797	Federalist	John Adams
2	John Adams	1797–1801	Federalist	Thomas Jefferson
3	Thomas Jefferson	1801–1809	Democratic-Republican	Aaron Burr (1801–1805), George Clinton (1805–1809)
4	James Madison	1809–1817	Democratic-Republican	George Clinton (1809–1812), none (1812–1813), Elbridge Gerry (1813–1814), none (1814–1817)
5	James Monroe	1817–1825	Democratic-Republican	Daniel D. Thompkins
6	John Q. Adams	1825–1829	Democratic-Republican	John C. Calhoun
7	Andrew Jackson	1829–1837	Democrat	John C. Calhoun (1829–1832), none (1832–1833), Martin Van Buren (1833–1837)
8	Martin Van Buren	1837–1841	Democrat	Richard M. Johnson
9	William H. Harrison	1841	Whig	John Tyler
10	John Tyler	1841–1845	Whig	none
11	James K. Polk	1845–1849	Democrat	George M. Dallas

	President	Term	Party	Vice President(s)
12	Zachary Taylor	1849–1850	Whig	Millard Fillmore
13	Millard Fillmore	1850–1853	Whig	none
14	Franklin Pierce	1853–1857	Democrat	William R. King (1853), none (1853–1857)
15	James Buchanan	1857–1861	Democrat	John C. Breckinridge
16	Abraham Lincoln	1861–1865	Republican	Hannibal Hamlin (1861–1865), Andrew Johnson (1865)
17	Andrew Johnson	1865–1869	Republican	none
18	Ulysses S. Grant	1869–1877	Republican	Schuyler Colfax (1869–1873), ◄ Henry Wilson (1873–1875), none (1875–1877)
19	Rutherford B. Hayes	1877–1881	Republican	William A. Wheeler
20	James A. Garfield	1881	Republican	Chester A. Arthur
21	Chester A. Arthur	1881–1885	Republican	none
22	Grover Cleveland	1885–1889	Democrat	Thomas A. Hendricks (1885), none (1885–1889)
23	Benjamin Harrison	1889–1893	Republican	Levi P. Morton
24	Grover Cleveland	1893–1897	Democrat	Adlai E. Stevenson

	President	Term	Party	Vice President(s)
25	William McKinley	1897–1901	Republican	Garret A. Hobart (1897–1899), none (1899–1901), ◀ Theodore Roosevelt (1901)
26	Theodore Roosevelt	1901–1909	Republican	none (1901–1905), Charles W. Fairbanks (1905–1909)
27	William H. Taft	1909–1913	Republican	James S. Sherman (1909–1912), none (1912–1913)
28	Woodrow Wilson	1913–1921	Democrat	Thomas R. Marshall
29	Warren G. Harding	1921–1923	Republican	Calvin Coolidge
30	Calvin Coolidge	1923–1929	Republican	none (1923–1925), Charles Dawes (1925–1929)
31	Herbert Hoover	1929–1933	Republican	Charles Curtis
32	Franklin D. Roosevelt	1933–1945	Democrat	John N. Garner (1933–1941), Henry A. Wallace (1941–1945), ◀ Harry S Truman (1945)
33	Harry S Truman	1945–1953	Democrat	none (1945–1949), Alben W. Barkley (1949–1953)

	President	Term	Party	Vice President(s)
34	Dwight D. Eisenhower	1953–1961	Republican	Richard Nixon
35	John F. Kennedy	1961–1963	Democrat	Lyndon B. Johnson
36	Lyndon B. Johnson	1963–1969	Democrat	none (1963–1965), Hubert H. Humphrey (1965–1969)
37	Richard Nixon	1969–1974	Republican	◄ Spiro T. Agnew (1969–1973), none (1973), Gerald R. Ford (1973–1974)
38	Gerald R. Ford	1974–1977	Republican	none (1974), Nelson A. Rockefeller (1974–1977)
39	Jimmy Carter	1977–1981	Democrat	Walter F. Mondale
40	Ronald Reagan	1981–1989	Republican	George Bush
41	George Bush	1989–1993	Republican	Dan Quayle
42	William J. Clinton	1993–2001	Democrat	Albert Gore
43	George W. Bush	2001–	Republican	Dick Cheney

Powers of the President

The president has both **formal** powers—those stated in the Constitution—and **implied** powers—those assumed based on the interpretation of the Constitution.

According to the Constitution, the president

★ commands the armed forces.

★ appoints the head of each executive department.

★ grants pardons for crimes other than **impeachment**.

★ makes treaties with the advice and consent of Congress.

★ nominates and appoints various positions, including ambassadors and Supreme Court justices, with the consent of Congress.

★ presents a State of the Union address to Congress, usually once a year in January.

★ hosts ambassadors and other representatives of foreign countries.

★ makes legislative recommendations to Congress.

★ takes care that all laws are faithfully executed.

Declaring War: Not a Presidential Power

The United States has not formally declared war since World War II. Under the U.S. Constitution (Article I, Section 8), Congress has sole power "to declare war." However, the Constitution also states in Article II, Section 2, that "the president shall be Commander in Chief of the Army and Navy of the United States." American presidents have used the implied powers of commander in chief to authorize military force abroad more than 225 times. Only on five occasions has Congress declared war—the War of 1812, the Mexican War, the Spanish-American War, World War I, and World War II.

Unlike the formal powers, the implied powers have been and continue to be disputed and debated. The implied powers are based on interpretations of the Constitution. Many of these powers apply to the extensive and vaguely defined presidential authority in international relations and to what **precedents** past presidents have set.

What Is Impeachment?

Sometimes presidents do things that, in the eyes of the people that they serve, are wrong. When this happens, the president may be impeached, or found guilty of doing something improper. The impeachment process starts with the House of Representatives. If two-thirds of the House members vote in favor of impeachment, the process moves on to the Senate, which must, in turn, find the individual guilty of wrongdoing by a two-thirds vote. Only then is the individual removed from office.

The impeachment process has been used against two presidents, but neither was removed from office. In 1868, President Andrew Johnson was impeached by the House for violating the Tenure of Office Act. This act states that a president cannot remove a federal official who has been approved by the Senate. The Senate, however, failed to impeach him by one vote.

In 1998, President William J. Clinton was found guilty by the House of two impeachment charges—**perjury** and **obstruction of justice**. The Senate, however, did not have enough votes to impeach him.

One other president came close to impeachment. President Richard Nixon chose to **resign** rather than face the impeachment process. Nixon was threatened with impeachment due to his role in covering up a break-in at the Democratic National Committee headquarters at the Watergate building in Washington, D.C., in 1974.

Richard Nixon leaves the White House by helicopter after his resignation.

Balancing the "Stool"

The Constitution provides checks and balances for the three branches of government. Each branch is able to examine and **amend**, within its **jurisdiction**, the actions of the other branches. In the executive branch, the president can **veto** bills that are passed by Congress and make appointments to the Supreme Court.

Line of Succession for President

Vice president
Speaker of the House of
    Representatives
President pro tempore
    of the Senate
Secretary of State
Secretary of the Treasury
Secretary of Defense
Attorney General
Secretary of the Interior
Secretary of Agriculture
Secretary of Commerce
Secretary of Labor
Secretary of Health and
    Human Services
Secretary of Housing and
    Urban Development
Secretary of Transportation
Secretary of Energy
Secretary of Education
Secretary of Veterans Affairs
Secretary of Homeland Security

Succeeding the President

Sometimes a president cannot complete his four-year term. If a president dies during his term or resigns from office, the vice president becomes president. If something happens to both the president and vice president, the Speaker of the House moves into the presidential role, and **succeeding** him is the president pro tempore of the Senate. The line of succession continues with the heads of the cabinet departments. The line of succession has changed several times. The Presidential Succession Act of 1947 determined the line of succession that we use today.

The Vice President

The vice president is part of the presidential team. He is elected at the same time as the president on the same party **ticket** and serves the same four-year term.

According to the Constitution, the vice president has two primary duties. He presides over the Senate, but he does not debate or vote, except in the case of a tie. The vice president also steps in when the president is disabled or unable to perform his duties. He automatically becomes president if there is a presidential death or resignation.

The president may ask the vice president to perform special duties, such as to represent the United States in trips abroad or to supervise special projects. Some vice presidents are more active than others.

Presidential candidates often select vice-presidential running mates to bring a balance to the ticket. The goal is to appeal to as many voters as possible.

The vice president has an office in the West Wing of the White House and also a set of offices in the Eisenhower Executive Office Building on the White House grounds.

Vice Presidents Who Became President During Their Successors' Terms

In 1963, President John F. Kennedy was assassinated in Dallas, Texas. While on board Air Force One, the official presidential jet, Vice President Lyndon B. Johnson was **sworn in** as president of the United States by a Texas judge.

Eight other vice presidents took the oath of office to become president in emergency situations.

★ John Tyler after William H. Harrison's death in 1841

★ Millard Fillmore after Zachary Taylor's death in 1850

★ Andrew Johnson after Abraham Lincoln's assassination in 1865

★ Chester A. Arthur after James A. Garfield's assassination in 1881

★ Theodore Roosevelt after William McKinley's assassination in 1901

★ Calvin Coolidge after Warren G. Harding's death in 1923

★ Harry S Truman after Franklin D. Roosevelt's death in 1945

★ Gerald R. Ford after Richard Nixon's resignation in 1974

Cabinet

The cabinet is an important group of advisors to the president. It is composed of the heads, or secretaries, of the executive departments. While they have no voting power and are not recognized by the Constitution of the United States, cabinet members are a critical component of the executive team. The members of the cabinet and their department duties are discussed in chapter 3.

Executive Office

The president surrounds himself with advisors who make up his executive staff. Its composition varies with each president. Some of these offices are the Council of Economic Advisers, the National Security Council, and the USA Freedom Corps. These and others are introduced in chapter 4.

Independent Agencies

In addition to the president's cabinet and executive office agencies and councils, the executive branch also includes independent agencies. These agencies are discussed in chapter 5.

White House

With the exception of George Washington, all the presidents have called the White House home during their time in office. Whitewashed in 1798 to protect the stone walls, the residence was burned by the British in 1814. The charred structure was restored in time for President James Monroe to move into it in 1817.

The White House has been enlarged and rebuilt over the years.

The president works in the Oval Office in the West Wing. He and his family live in private quarters on the second and third floors of the building.

While it is the president's home and office, the White House is also the "people's home." The staterooms of the complex are open to the public. They include the State Dining Room, the East Room, the Red Room, the Blue Room, and the Green Room. Would you like to tour the White House? The tours begin at **www.whitehouse.gov/ kids/tour** or **www.whitehouse.gov/ history/whtour**.

The Green Room

Camp David

Everyone needs to relax, including the president and his family. Nestled in the Catoctin Mountains of Maryland is Camp David. It was originally called Shangri-La by President Franklin D. Roosevelt when it opened in 1942. In 1953, the name was changed to Camp David by President Dwight D. Eisenhower to honor his grandson. Today it serves as a vacation home and a working retreat for the president.

First Lady

When citizens of the United States elect a president, they often receive a package deal. The president's wife, known as the First Lady, plays an important role. She is the first hostess, actively involved in presidential social gatherings.

The First Lady has her own office in the White House. She and her staff are located in the East Wing.

The First Lady usually chooses causes or issues to support during her husband's time in office. Hillary Rodham Clinton, wife of William J. Clinton, worked on health-reform issues. Barbara Bush, wife of George Bush, was a promoter of literacy, while Nancy Reagan, wife of Ronald Reagan, directed her energies toward the nation's veterans, seniors, drug and alcohol abuse, and young performers. Many First Ladies promoted the arts.

Will the husband of the first female president be called "The First Man"? What will his roles officially be? Time will tell!

The "First" First Lady

While numerous First Ladies filled the shoes of presidential hostess, it wasn't until 1877 when the term *First Lady* was first used. Rutherford B. Hayes referred to his wife, Lucy, as the First Lady in his inauguration speech.

Not all First Ladies were wives. Sometimes sisters, nieces, friends, and children stepped in to fill the role because of family circumstances.

Lucy Hayes

Chapter 3

A Cabinet of Advisors

Backdoor Politics

President Andrew Jackson relied on his cabinet of advisors and wanted to meet with them on a regular basis. But those not invited to these meetings felt shut out. So participants entered through the private back door of the White House. The secret gatherers were called the Kitchen Cabinet, inferring that they met in secrecy in the kitchen quarters. With only four cabinet members, it was easy for them to "sneak" inside!

Today the president's cabinet meets openly. In 2003, President George W. Bush's cabinet was composed of the vice president, the attorney general, and 14 department heads. President Bush also included the chief of staff, the administrator of the Environmental Protection Agency, the director of the Office of Management and Budget, the director of the National Drug Control Policy, and the U.S. Trade representative. Like a CEO of a corporation relies on the advice from his board of directors, the president depends on his cabinet to advise him.

President Clinton (third from left) holds a meeting in the Cabinet Room at the White House, 1999.

25

The president selects his cabinet members at the beginning of his term. Because of the Constitution's checks and balances, the Senate must approve each department head.

Members of the cabinet specialize in selected areas of government. They bring expertise to the executive branch. They brief the president on world and national events and suggest policies. They present information and options to the president to help him in his daily work.

Agriculture

President Abraham Lincoln convinced Congress to establish the U.S. Department of Agriculture (USDA) in 1862. He called it the "People's Department." At that time, farmers in need of seeds and information to grow crops comprised 48 percent of the population.

Today the role of the Department of Agriculture has grown. It is involved in school breakfast and lunch programs. It ensures reasonable incomes for farmers and reasonably priced farm products for consumers. It works to combat hunger, sets guidelines for Americans' nutrition, and oversees programs such as food stamps and the WIC (women, infants, and children) program.

Commerce

Founded in 1903, the Department of Commerce is responsible for job creation and economic growth. When you hear statistics on the news about new home sales, the job market, and general economic growth or decline, they were usually released by the Department of Commerce. Every ten years, the U.S. Census Bureau (parented by the Department of Commerce) surveys the country's citizens and releases figures on the growing and shifting population.

New inventors register their ideas with the Patent and Trademark Office, which is administered by the Department of Commerce. The Department of Commerce is even responsible for your daily weather forecast, as the National Weather Service is part of this department.

Defense

Originally called the Department of War, the Department of Defense directs the activities of the army, navy, air force, and marines. The Department of Defense oversees the acquiring and building of weapons, developing and protecting military communications, and gathering military intelligence.

The Joint Chiefs of Staff, part of the Department of Defense, consists of high-ranking officials from all branches of the armed forces. The members serve as military advisors to the president, the National Security Council, and the secretary of defense.

The Pentagon

The Defense Department is well known for the shape of its building, a pentagon. Built in just two years during World War II, the Pentagon houses 23,000 employees and is considered to be the largest office building in the world.

Education

The Department of Education helps to determine what you learn in school. Founded in 1979 as a cabinet department, it was first created as a non-cabinet post in 1867.

The primary goals of the Department of Education are to ensure improved public school education and to promote educational opportunities for all U.S. citizens.

Energy

While the Department of Energy oversees energy use in the country, it has other concerns too. Its mission is "to advance the national economic and energy security of the United States, to promote scientific and technological innovation in support of that mission, and to ensure the environmental cleanup of the national nuclear weapons complex."

Health and Human Services

The Department of Health and Human Services was established to protect the health of all Americans and to provide essential human services. It provides medical insurance for elderly, disabled, and low-income people. The Food and Drug Administration oversees the food we eat and the medicines we take. The Centers for Disease Control and Prevention tracks outbreaks of illness.

Homeland Security

The lives of all Americans changed on September 11, 2001, when terrorists attacked the United States. To protect the nation against additional threats to the homeland, President George W. Bush brought together 22 previously separate **domestic** agencies and placed them under one department head. Among those agencies are the U.S. Customs Service, the Immigration and Naturalization Service, and the Federal Emergency Management Agency (FEMA). The Secret Service and the Coast Guard are also part of the department.

While the Department of Homeland Security is responsible for security of the country, it also assists in times of natural disasters, such as hurricanes and floods.

Red Light–Green Light: The Homeland Security Advisory System

To keep American citizens informed of the current terrorist-threat level to the country, the Department of Homeland Security created a system of color codes in 2002.

Green = Low   Orange = High
Blue = Guarded   Red = Severe
Yellow = Elevated

SEVERE
Severe Risk of Terrorist Attacks

HIGH
High Risk of Terrorist Attacks

ELEVATED
Significant Risk of Terrorist Attacks

GUARDED
General Risk of Terrorist Attacks

LOW
Low Risk of Terrorist Attacks

Housing and Urban Development (HUD)

The Department of Housing and Urban Development was created in 1965 to assist families with their housing needs. The department works to increase the affordability and quality of housing and helps cities improve their **impoverished** neighborhoods. In July 2001, the department reactivated the Interagency Council on the Homeless to help those with no homes.

The Interior

In 1849, Congress created the Department of the Interior. Its primary purpose is to take care of the country's internal affairs. It provides programs for Native Americans, manages the country's national parks, and works to conserve and develop the nation's natural resources.

The department's role in government has changed as new departments have been added. A few milestones are worth noting in the department's history.

★ 1872—Yellowstone is named the country's first national park.

★ 1903—President Theodore Roosevelt establishes the first National Wildlife Refuge at Pelican Island, Florida.

* 1916—President Wilson signs legislation creating The National Park Service.

* 1935—The Bureau of Reclamation completes construction of the Hoover Dam.

* 1995—Gray wolves are reintroduced to Yellowstone National Park.

Hoover Dam at the Nevada–Arizona border

National Capital Parks

Established in 1965, the National Capital Parks, part of the Department of the Interior, oversees memorial sites in Washington, D.C. These include the Washington Monument, the Lincoln Memorial, the Vietnam Veterans Memorial, the Franklin D. Roosevelt Memorial, Ford's Theatre National Historic Site, and many more. Each year the National Capital Parks also issues permits for thousands of special events on the National Mall, a large, grassy park area that stretches for almost ten blocks. More than ten million people visit these attractions each year.

The Lincoln Memorial

Justice

The Attorney General is the head of the Department of Justice. He is the only cabinet department head not called a secretary.

President George Washington named the first attorney general in 1789, but the Justice Department was not established until 1870. Since then, the department has grown into the largest law office in the country. It is responsible for enforcing all federal laws. It also provides the president and other department heads with legal advice. Today it manages the work of over 30 agencies, including the Drug Enforcement Administration (DEA), the Federal Bureau of Investigation (FBI), and the Bureau of Alcohol, Tobacco, Firearms, and Explosives (ATF).

Wanted: Good Cyber Citizens

Rules, rules, everywhere rules—even in cyberspace! One of the goals of the Department of Justice is to ensure that everyone—especially children—has a positive and safe online experience. The Department of Justice shares cyber-safe information on its Web site at **www.cybercrime.gov/rules/ kidinternet.htm**.

Labor

At one time, labor issues were the responsibility of the Department of the Interior. In 1913, Congress established the Department of Labor. According to the department's mission statement, it is responsible for "promoting the welfare of the job seekers, wage earners, and retirees of the United States." The department strives to improve working conditions and opportunities for employment.

The Department of Labor was the first department to have a female secretary. In 1933, President Franklin D. Roosevelt appointed Frances Perkins to the position.

Child Labor: For Some It Was More Than Doing Chores

Imagine being 11 years old, and instead of going to school, you spend your day working in a factory for minimal pay. At one time in this country, many children did not go to school. Their families needed them to earn money. The conditions were horrendous. The children's futures were dismal.

Today, laws prevent young children from working and older children from working long hours. Children cannot work in jobs that are considered hazardous by the department. Their education must come first.

If you want to have a job while you're in school, you may need to obtain a work permit. It's granted by the Department of Labor.

State

Created in 1789, the Department of State is the oldest cabinet department. Even though it has the word *state* in its name, it does not control the state in which you live. The Department of State is responsible for communicating and coordinating efforts with other governments. It works hard to resolve conflicts in other parts of the world.

In addition to being the first cabinet department, the Department of State holds the distinction for two other firsts. Madeleine Albright, the secretary of state from 1997 to 2001, was the first woman to hold the position. The first African American to head this department was Colin Powell, appointed in 2001.

Transportation

The Department of Transportation is responsible for every federal transportation system in the United States. Congress established this department in 1966. Its mission is to "serve the United States by ensuring a fast, safe, efficient, accessible, and convenient transportation system that meets our vital national interests and enhances the quality of life of the American people, today and into the future."

When terrorists attacked the United States on September 11, 2001, it was this department, working with President George W. Bush, that decided to close all of the country's airports and increase security measures at train and bus stations.

The Treasury

When people hear the word *treasury*, they think of money, and that is the primary focus of this department. The Department of Treasury oversees the production of paper money, coins, and postage stamps. It manages federal finances and government accounts. It collects money through its Internal Revenue Service (IRS).

Did you know that the Secret Service, the agency that protects the president, was part of the Treasury Department until recently? During the Civil War great amounts of counterfeit money were being made and circulated. The Secret Service, a federal law enforcement agency, investigated this currency fraud. It wasn't until 1906 that the service began protecting the president and his family. In 2001, the Secret Service became part of the Department of Homeland Security.

Pennies made at the Denver mint

Veterans Affairs (VA)

The Department of Veterans Affairs takes care of our country's veterans and their dependents. This department provides assistance for health care, rehabilitation, financial aid, and burial.

Did you know that

★ almost three-quarters of the 26 million veterans currently alive served during a war or an official period of conflict?

★ 70 million people—veterans, family members, or survivors of veterans—in the United States are eligible for VA benefits and services?

★ the last dependent of a Revolutionary War veteran died in 1911?

★ since the first GI Bill began in 1944, more than 21 million veterans, service members, and family members have received $75 billion for education and training?

★ there are 163 VA hospitals in the country?

★ the first liver transplant in the world was performed by a VA surgeon-researcher?

★ the Seattle Foot was developed by the VA? The mechanism allows people with amputations to run and jump.

★ the VA has provided more than 8.1 million headstones and markers for veterans' graves since 1973?

Sitka National Cemetary, Sitka, Alaska

Chapter 4

The Executive Office

A s the CEO of a powerful nation, the president needs a strong staff to organize and guide him. We live in a time of change. While our country is based on the same principles as it was 200 years ago, today it does not have the same concerns that it did then. Most of the offices, councils, and boards within the Executive Office were created by **executive order** or by acts of Congress.

With each president comes a new set of challenges. The president's Executive Office and staff reflect those challenges. After his inauguration in 2001, President George W. Bush issued his first executive order. It created an executive office, the Office of Faith-Based and Community Initiatives, to reflect the needs of the country at that time.

Council of Economic Advisers

The Council of Economic Advisers (CEA) was first established in 1946. Composed of three key members, the CEA advises the president on issues impacting the financial health of the country.

Council on Environmental Quality

Everything you do affects the environment—positively or negatively. Making the shoes you wear, growing the food you eat, publishing the books you read, or traveling from your home to your school has an environmental impact. We live in a beautiful country. The president and his Council on Environmental Quality develop policies that will keep it that way!

National Economic Council

The National Economic Council watches activities that affect economic programs in the United States and abroad. The areas it monitors include agriculture, commerce, energy, financial markets, fiscal policy, health care, labor, and Social Security.

National Security Council

The National Security Council is the president's main forum for discussing national security and foreign policy issues with senior national-security advisors and cabinet officials. Because of the council's importance, the president himself chairs the council. Members of the council include the vice president, the secretary of state, the secretary of the treasury, the secretary of defense, and the assistant to the president for National Security Affairs. The chairman of the Joint Chiefs of Staff serves as the military advisor to the council, and the director of the Central Intelligence Agency is the intelligence advisor. Depending on the issues to be discussed, other secretaries and directors may be asked to attend the working sessions.

President Johnson (second from right) meets with the National Security Council, 1964

Office of Administration

The Office of Administration, established by executive order in 1977, provides administrative services to the president and all groups within the president's Executive Office. These support services can include financial management and information technology support, human resources management, library and research assistance, facilities management, procurement (contracting for the supply of goods and services), printing and graphics support, security, and mail and messenger operations.

Office of Faith-Based and Community Initiatives

President George W. Bush created the Office of Faith-Based and Community Initiatives when he took office in 2001. The goal of the office is to allow community and church programs to partner with the federal government to help those in need—such as at-risk youth, former criminals, the homeless and hungry, substance abusers, individuals with HIV/AIDS, and families moving from public assistance programs into the working sector. The government provides funding through grants for qualified programs. The office holds workshops throughout the nation to train community program leaders.

Getting on the Right Path: Helping At-Risk Youth

To help young people, especially those less fortunate, the federal government has created and/or provided money for special programs. Many children attend Head Start as preschoolers. Runaway teens often turn to shelters for help. Parents seek help from organizations when adopting a child. Does your school have programs about prevention of drug and alcohol abuse? All these programs may have been funded through grants sponsored by the Office of Faith-Based and Community Initiatives.

Office of Management and Budget

Everyone has a budget, including the government! The Office of Management and Budget is responsible for operating the government within certain monetary guidelines. The office's primary mission is to assist the president in preparing the national budget. It also manages the use of funds in executive-branch departments.

Office of National Drug Control Policy

The goals of the Office of National Drug Control Policy are to reduce illegal drug use and to stop illegal drug manufacturing and selling. Through its efforts, the council tries to prevent drug-related crime and violence. It also educates the public about drug-related health consequences.

Connecting Electronically with Citizens

Just like a progressive company, your government operates a Web site. Actually, it operates many, as most departments and agencies have their own sites. To start your cyber adventure, go to **www.firstgov.gov**.

Drugged Driving

According to a 2003 analysis of Monitoring the Future data, one in every six high school seniors has driven while under the influence of marijuana. In the same study, these students shared that 38,000 of them had had an accident while under the influence of the drug.

USA Freedom Corps

Everyone can be a volunteer, including you! How can you help? You could read to younger children, help an older neighbor, take care of a stray animal, or donate your used toys, books, or clothes. You can find more ideas on the corps' Web site at **www.usafreedomcorps.gov**.

White House Military Office

The president is an active leader. While he does spend time in the White House, he also travels around the country and the world on national business. The White House Military Office is responsible for coordinating the president's travel plans. The office oversees Air Force One, the presidential jet; Camp David, the presidential retreat; Marine One, the presidential helicopter; and the presidential limousine. The office even cooks! Food service for the president, his family, and guests is one of the office's responsibilities.

Air Force One: An Office with Wings

The president can take his office and staff with him when he travels. Air Force One is the name given to the presidential jet. Air Force One can fly halfway around the world without refueling. It can carry more than 70 passengers.

To learn more about the Executive Office and its numerous councils, explore the White House Web site: **www.whitehouse.gov/government/eop.html**.

Chapter 5

Independent Agencies

In addition to the president's cabinet and Executive Office agencies and councils, the executive branch also includes independent agencies. Congress created independent agencies to address specific concerns and advise the president. Currently there are more than 135 independent agencies. Here are some of them.

★ Central Intelligence Agency (CIA)

★ Commission on Civil Rights

★ Environmental Protection Agency (EPA)

★ Equal Employment Opportunity Commission (EEOC)

◄ ★ National Aeronautics and Space Administration (NASA)

★ National Endowment for the Arts/Humanities

First Peace Corps volunteers to leave for overseas duty

★ National Science Foundation

★ Peace Corps

★ Small Business Administration

★ Smithsonian Institution ➤

★ Social Security Administration

★ United States Postal Service

For a complete listing of current independent agencies, go to **www.firstgov.gov/Agencies/Federal/ Independent.shtml**.

★ ★ ★ ★ ★

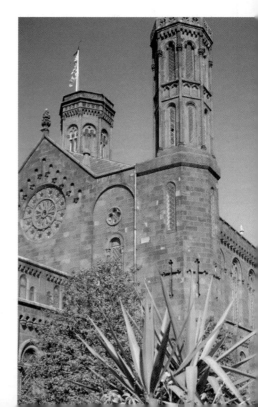

Growing Up: Small Business and the Young Entrepreneur

Big is not always best! The federal government provides resource information and funding opportunities for small business owners to help them launch new business ideas and grow in their established businesses. The Small Business Administration even offers start-up information for young **entrepreneurs**. For example, what is a business plan? What kinds of businesses can teenagers create? Where can young entrepreneurs meet? Answers to these questions and many more can be found on the SBA site, **app1.sba.gov/faqs/faqindex.cfm?areaID=30**.

One Generation Helping Another

Before Social Security benefits were available for older Americans, several generations in one family may have lived together. Working parents cared not only for their own children but also for their retired parents.

Today, one generation still cares for another, but in a different way. Parents who work pay into the Social Security System. Older generations collect Social Security benefits monthly.

With great foresight, the framers of the Constitution created a government that has persevered for more than 225 years. The country has more than tripled in size since 1776, and the population has grown and diversified. Yet the three branches of government have worked together to maintain the balanced government that the Founders had planned.

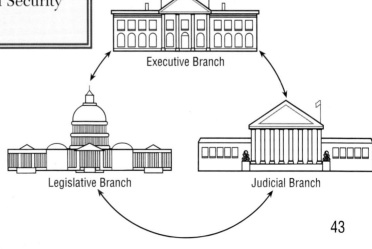

Executive Branch

Legislative Branch

Judicial Branch

43

Internet Connections and Related Readings

for the Executive Branch

www.whitehouse.gov

This is a great site for learning about the executive branch. Explore the site to find out about the president, the vice president, the First Lady, the cabinet, the Executive Office, the independent agencies, and the history of the White House. Read biographies of former presidents and First Ladies. Virtual tours of the White House are also available.

www.firstgov.gov

This is the "official gateway" to the U.S. government. Whatever you want or need from the U.S. government is here. Find a treasure of online information as well as a link just for kids.

bensguide.gpo.gov

Enter Ben's Guide to U.S. Government for Kids and explore the branches of government and other interesting topics that relate to the U.S. government.

www.grolier.com/presidents/preshome.html

The Grolier Online Encyclopedia presents The American Presidency. This is an exclusive history of presidents, the presidency, politics, and related subjects.

www.umkc.edu/imc/prestriv.htm
www.factmonster.com/spot/prestrivia1.html

These two sites are filled with interesting information and trivia about the presidents. For example, did you know that Vice President John Tyler was on his knees playing marbles when he learned that he had become president?

★　★　★　★　★　★　★

Our Constitution by Linda Carlson Johnson. This book describes the creation of the document, which sets out the rules of government for our country. Millbrook, 1992. [RL 5.6 IL 3–6] (4695306 HB)

Our Presidency by Karen Spies. This book from the *I Know America* series describes how the office of the presidency has grown and changed in this country and takes a look at a typical day in a president's life. Millbrook, 1994. [RL 4 IL 2–6] (4930901 PB 4930906 CC)

Presidential Pet "Tails" by Kathleen Muldoon. Read about the pets of eight presidents, some of which became as famous as their owners. Perfection Learning Corporation, 2002. [RL 2.9 IL 2–6] (3243601 PB 3243602 CC)

So You Want to Be President? by Judith St. George. This collection of stories tells about 41 men who have risen to one of the most powerful positions in the world. Putnam, 2000. [RL 4 IL 3–6] (4374201 PB)

The letters *RL* in the brackets indicate the reading level of the book listed. *IL* indicates the approximate interest level. Perfection Learning's catalog numbers are included for your ordering convenience. *HB* indicates hardcover, *PB* indicates paperback, and *CC* indicates Cover Craft.

Glossary

amend (uh MEND) to revise or alter something

checks and balances (cheks and BAL en suhz) limits placed on all branches of government by giving each the right to amend (see separate glossary entry) acts of the other branches

confirmed (kuhn FERMD) approved

discontent (dis kuhn TENT) feeling dissatisfied with a situation

domestic (duh MES tik) relating to the internal affairs of a nation

entrepreneur (ahn truh pruh NER) someone who sets up and finances a new business to make a profit

executive branch (ig ZEK you tiv branch) part of the government that enforces the laws of the country

executive order (ig ZEK you tiv OR der) rule or act that has the status of a law

formal (FOR muhl) done or carried out as established by prescribed rules

impeachment (im PEECH muhnt) act of charging a government official with wrongdoing and possibly removing him or her from office

implied (im PLEYED) understood or suggested without being stated

impoverished (im PAHV rishd) poor and run-down

judicial branch (jyou DISH uhl branch) part of the government that interprets laws and the Constitution

jurisdiction (jer uhs DIK shuhn) power or right to exercise control

legislative branch (LEJ uhs lay tiv branch) part of the government that writes and passes laws

obstruction of justice (ahb STRUHK shuhn uhv JUHS tis) interference with the law process or an investigation

perjury (PER juh ree) telling a lie or omitting information under oath

policy (PAHL uh see) program of actions

preamble (PREE am buhl) section at the beginning of an important formal (see separate glossary entry) document that explains the purpose

precedent (PRES uh duhnt) earlier happening of something similar

resign (ri ZEYEN) to give up a job voluntarily

succeed (suhk SEED) to follow somebody occupying a post or position

sworn in (sworn in) given the oath of office

ticket (TIK uht) list of candidates put forward by one party or group in an election

transportation (tranz per TAY shuhn) business of carrying people or goods from one place to another

veteran (VET uh ruhn) person who served in the armed forces

veto (VEE toh) power or right to reject something

Index